AUSTRALIA'S
MOST

ADORABLE

ANIMAL
TALES

First published as *A Wombat in My Drawer* by Affirm Press in 2016
This revised and updated edition published by Affirm Press in 2021
28 Thistlethwaite Street, South Melbourne,
Boonwurrung Country, VIC 3205
affirmpress.com.au

Text © Ros Almond 2016 and Affirm Press 2021
Internal design © Affirm Press 2016
Typesetting by Post Pre-press Group 2021

 A catalogue record for this book is available from the National Library of Australia

ISBN: 9781922626189 (hardback)

Cover and book design by Karen Wallis
Cover image © David Caird/Newspix
Printed and bound in China by C&C Offset Printing Co., Ltd

AUSTRALIA'S MOST
ADORABLE
ANIMAL TALES

MERV LAMINGTON

Affirm
press

INTRODUCTION

Australia is famous for a lot of things – incredible landscapes, beautiful beaches, friendly people and weird slang words – but nothing says 'Aussie' quite like our animals. From Skippy the kangaroo to Dundee's crocodiles and the ridiculous number of deadly creatures we have to deal with, when the rest of the world thinks 'down under', they think animals.

So who'd have thought our animals could be even funnier, crazier, sillier and cuter than any of us realised? Every day there are adorable critters getting into scrapes, going on wild and unexpected adventures, and making unusual friends. There are also some amazing humans working hard to look after these animals and ensure the best possible future for our wildlife and environment.

In celebration of all these fascinating creatures, the team at Affirm Press have collected some of the very best animal tales from across the country, adopting the nom de plume of Merv Lamington to represent our collective efforts.

We hope you enjoy reading it as much as we enjoyed creating it.

SMUDGE, the SUGAR GLIDER

Smudge was saved by an animal rescue organisation when he was a tiny joey. At the time he was a bit of a sad mess, weighing only 32 grams. A well-meaning person spotted the sweet creature and thought they'd adopt him, but without the right knowledge and care, it's quite difficult to ensure the survival of baby native animals – especially ones as small as Smudge.

Sugar gliders generally stay in their mother's pouch for about ten weeks, but they aren't completely independent until they are between seven and ten months old. They're not really able to survive on their own without proper nutrients and care for quite some time. Luckily for Smudge, the Wildlife Information, Rescue and Education Service (WIRES) took him in and he received the necessary intensive care. After two and a half months, Smudge was a lot stronger and was able to be released into the wild, joining a group of older sugar gliders.

Although they're super cute, these creatures are pretty fragile, so it's best to leave their care to the experts.

LITTLE DEVILS

Young Tasmanian devils may be sweet-looking creatures, but they wouldn't make the most pleasant dinner guests. These stocky little carnivores like to chill out during the day and scavenge for food at night, and they eat absolutely everything they find: bones, fur, the whole shebang. It's gross, but at least they leave minimal clean-up.

Tassie devils almost became extinct during the early 20th century when farmers who were determined to protect their livestock attempted to eradicate the scavengers. In fact, Tasmanian devils are far more into leftovers than fresh kills and very rarely take their own prey.

Luckily, devil numbers have grown since they became a protected species in 1941. But during the 1990s, Devil Facial Tumour Disease (DFTD) was recognised as having a major impact on the population. To ensure the species' survival, a number of programs were developed to try to find a cure for the disease, limit its spread and maintain healthy populations. Aussie Ark in Barrington Tops National Park, New South Wales, plays an important role in a strategic breeding program of healthy devils to maintain a genetically diverse population. This adorable crew are part of that program. And while they're working that whole 'butter wouldn't melt in my mouth' look, you probably still shouldn't invite them to any fancy dinners.

did you know?

Tasmanian devils have been reintroduced to the Australian mainland! In 2020, the conservation group Aussie Ark released twenty-six Tasmanian Devils into a 500-hectare wildlife sanctuary in Barrington Tops National Park, New South Wales. A few tears may have been shed at the reintroduction.

CUTE CHICK

In a story reminiscent of the literary classic *Are You My Mother?* by PD Eastman, a tiny, adorable tawny frogmouth was blown out of its nest and went for a ride in a cherry picker to try to find its mum.

The chick, who was barely bigger than a fifty cent coin, was found by a local resident and taken to WIRES Northern Rivers, where the little tacker was checked over and cared for until he was ready to be returned to the trees. But this was a bigger task than WIRES anticipated, since the nest was a fair bit higher than anyone could reach. So Steve Cubis, a local tree feller, offered his cherry picker to take the chick home.

WIRES was very impressed and grateful for the offer: 'Looking down from the basket we couldn't help but marvel at this enormous piece of machinery delivering such a tiny parcel such a small distance. How amazing that WIRES support is so strong from a non-member who took time and effort to deliver a service that we could not have managed without.'

In an ending that's enough to restore your faith in humanity, Steve found the nest, complete with the tawny's siblings and parents, and safely delivered the fluffball home.

It really is good to have friends in high places.

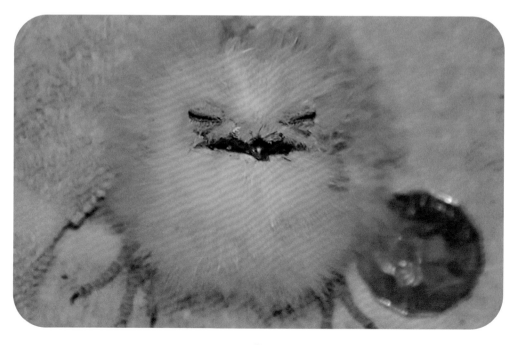

did you know?

There are around fourteen related species of tree kangaroo, ten of which live in New Guinea. Australia has two: the Lumholtz's and the Bennett's tree kangaroo. Both live in Queensland in pretty limited areas, and their ongoing survival depends on us preserving their natural environments.

Is it a bird? no, it's a TREE KANGAROO

Lucy the Lumholtz's tree kangaroo is from the rainforests of the Atherton Tablelands, and like any member of her species she's a funny-looking little thing that seems to be about 50 per cent kangaroo, 50 per cent possum and 100 per cent gorgeous. Tree kangaroos live in small groups, but generally like to keep to themselves.

Lucy was brought to a rescue centre in Queensland after she hopped into someone's house. Her vision isn't great, so if she was returned to the rainforest she would struggle to survive. Instead, she lives quite happily at the Wildlife Habitat in Port Douglas, and has become close to another Lumholtz's tree kangaroo called Colin. They live together in the park where they help to increase awareness of the potential vulnerability of these cute critters and the importance of preserving their limited natural environments to ensure their continuation as a species.

As adorable as this is, please do not knit a penguin a jumper. Instead, we suggest that you donate to the Penguin Foundation to ensure that the high-quality care of these little penguins can continue.

PENGUINS in JUMPERS

In 2000, an oil spill off the south coast of Australia affected Phillip Island's little penguin population. The oil coated and matted the penguins' feathers so that the birds were unable to fluff up, dry off and keep warm.

The penguins' reaction was to try to preen their feathers, but since ingesting even a small amount of the oil could kill the birds, the preening had to be stopped. Eventually, the Phillip Island Penguin Foundation discovered a solution: covering the penguins' feathers with little woollen jumpers. Genius!

Because it was such an adorable solution (and penguin jumpers don't take anywhere near as long to knit as human jumpers) the foundation was soon swamped with more tiny knitwear than they could possibly need. In 2019, they received so many jumpers that they closed the program. The excess jumpers were used to dress toy penguins, which were then sold to raise funds for a new wildlife clinic with updated facilities and cleaning technologies. And, even better, no penguins will be going cold anytime soon.

DUSTY the KANGAROO

Dusty's family wasn't like most kangaroo families: it was made up of a mix of canines, humans and, of course, one little marsupial ... who thought he was a dog.

Dusty joined the Stewart family after his mum was killed in a car accident. Luckily, Ashley and Felicity Stewart found him on the side of the road and decided to take him home. They fed him and took care of him, and over time the joey grew strong and healthy. He lived on the back veranda of the family home with Lilly the golden retriever and Rosie the border collie, who were more than happy to share their space with the new recruit. Dusty also joined the dogs in the back of the ute for drives around the property, and he tried to steal their treats. He loved pats and cuddles so much that it was easy to forget he wasn't a dog! He even wore a collar. Although, that was because kangaroos are super quiet and without the reflective collar the family couldn't find Dusty in the dark.

Dusty had a special relationship with Lilly – in fact, Ashley reckons that

Dusty thought Lilly was his mum. He followed her around and got a bit antsy if she went off on adventures without him.

While Dusty was free to explore the farm as he pleased, he always chose to come back to his bed on the veranda.

Dusty's story proves that some young animals can adapt well to new lifestyles, as long as they're in safe and loving environments. If Dusty had been returned to the wild, he probably would have struggled, but there's no doubt he did rather nicely as part of the Stewart family. His rescue shows how important it is to carefully check Australian marsupials after they've been involved in accidents with vehicles, because it might just be a mother with an orphaned joey. Most of the time these rescued animals are best taken to the nearest wildlife centre, but since a lot of places in Australia are too remote to have a centre nearby, occasionally these survivors become the responsibility of their rescuer.

tinder

Pat, 30

SWIPE RIGHT, FOR SURE

Patrick was perhaps the most unique wombat out there. He was, after all, the only wombat with a Tinder account!

Finding a partner in life isn't easy. Patrick wasn't the most assertive wombat at the disco, and when it came to the ladies he was often muscled out by the competition. Male wombats have to be quite aggressive to catch the attention of a mate and Patrick, being a rather sensitive and sophisticated fellow, wasn't one to get into a scuffle. So, he took the search online.

According to Julia Leonard at the Ballarat Wildlife Park, Patrick was 'after someone who enjoys late nights, especially dusk and dawn, can dig a good hole and enjoys feeding him carrots.'

Patrick's impressive age made him (as far as we know) the oldest living common wombat in the world, and he also happened to be one of the largest. Although his search failed to yield results, Patrick's bachelor lifestyle still gave him a long and happy thirty-one years.

Kangaroos may well be the go-to Australian mascot, but there's one underrated marsupial that we think could well rival the roo for athletic skill (and general awesomeness) and it's the humble wombat. These stocky little creatures may look slow and steady, but that cute waddle hides an ability to run up to 40 kilometres per hour. To put that in perspective, the human foot speed world record is 44.72 kilometres per hour, so if you were to race a wombat over 100 metres there's a good chance you'd lose (unless you're Usain Bolt, of course).

But the cool qualities of the wombat don't end there: they are also built to be the perfect digging machine. They create huge underground systems of tunnels and chambers, and if they need to escape down their burrows to avoid danger, they've got hard bums that are so tough, few predators can get past them. And it gets even more impressive, because if a predator tries to crawl over the top of the wombat, it will give one big, powerful push and crush the silly intruder against the top of the burrow. In other words, don't mess with a wombat.

BAZZ gets a BUZZ OUTTA BEEKEEPING

While working dogs are pretty common in Australia, they don't usually need to wear a uniform to get their job done. But Bazz's career is a bit different to that of the average working dog. The labrador lives with his owner, Josh, at an apiary in Tintinara, South Australia, and he's been specially trained to sniff out American foulbrood – a disease that wipes out bee larvae and messes with honey production.

Sniffer dogs are very helpful to humans (unless those humans have just got off a flight from Amsterdam), because their sense of smell is so strong they can detect odours that we can't even imagine. Labradors' noses, for example, have around 220 million olfactory receptors compared to the five million in a human nose.

By sniffing rather than breathing regularly, dogs are able to direct odours straight into a specialised region of their brain. Each additional sniff adds up to trigger the dog's olfactory receptors and help it identify the scent. This all means that dogs smell much better than humans. (Wait a second ...)

Bazz is the first Australian dog to be carefully trained to work in apiaries, and his incredibly perceptive sense of smell means that he's able to detect the disease early, before it destroys any larvae. It takes Bazz less than an hour to check the same number of beehives that five human apiarists need a whole three days to check. Clearly, he is far better at this part of being a beekeeper than any human.

There are other apiary dogs just like Bazz sniffing out foulbrood in parts of the USA, but the winters are so cold and snowy there the bees hibernate, allowing their four-legged protectors to do their jobs in peace. There's not as much snow in South Australia, and to smell whether or not the bees are infected, Bazz has to get pretty close to the hives. At the start, the poor fella kept getting stung so Josh designed a special suit for his canine co-worker to protect him and to give him that extra dash of style. Bazz took a while to get used to his new outfit, but with his suit on he can now do his job safely.

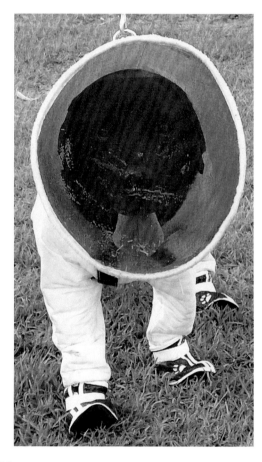

PUGGLE POWER

Leo the baby echidna was brought into the Healesville Sanctuary after being found, at only one month old, in a garden bed at Badger Creek, Victoria. When echidnas are babies (known as puggles), they don't have any of their characteristic spikes and can't even open their eyes, so while they're very cute, they also look a bit like they're made from Play-Doh covered in the skin of an earthworm. Leo was also tiny, weighing only 110 grams – about as much as a tomato. A little pink earthworm Play-Doh tomato? Absolutely adorable.

Echidnas, like platypuses, are a type of mammal called a monotreme. They lay eggs, like reptiles, but are warm-blooded and drink milk, just like every other mammal. The milk is excreted by the mother through little pad openings on her stomach, which her babies can suck up with their strange mouths. Echidnas have snouts with long, sticky tongues that allow them to collect insects and worms when they're old enough. They don't have any teeth, so their strong tongues are important for helping them crush up food inside their mouths. It makes drinking an interesting procedure. Lisa and Kelly, two keepers at Healesville Sanctuary, had to feed Leo milk off the palms of their hands so that the puggle could drink it.

Echidna puggles are weaned when they're about seven months old, and they usually stay pretty close to their mums until they're about a year old.

Because of this, Leo needed to be looked after for a while to make sure he would be strong enough to survive on his own.

Leo grew bigger and bigger every day, and soon started growing his fur and spines. He now looks less like a worm and more like the pine cone-shaped echidnas we know and love.

did you know?

Want a cool Aussie animal as a pet? There are a range of views on whether keeping native animals as pets is a good idea or not. On one hand, it means less culling, and it could help to preserve vulnerable populations. It would also minimise the number of dogs and cats kept as pets. On the other hand, some of these animals struggle in domestic environments. They require additional care and a long-term commitment from owners. It's an interesting and important debate.

SUPERDOG and the ORPHANED JOEY

Dogs sometimes get a bad rap when it comes to their effect on native animals, to the point where they've been banned from Australian national parks to ensure the protection of wildlife. Sometimes, though, dogs prove that they're capable of a lot more than instinctive aggression against our local fauna.

Rex, a German shorthaired pointer cross, performed a life-saving rescue mission near his home in Bells Beach. After discovering a kangaroo that had been killed by a car, Rex became preoccupied with the roo. While his owner, Leonie Allan, was worried Rex had found a snake, it turned out that he had found something less dangerous and much more adorable.

He'd sensed something wasn't right and carefully rescued a little joey from its mother's pouch.

The ten-year-old pooch carried the four-month-old joey in his mouth so gently that it remained cool, calm and completely unharmed. The pair got along swimmingly and were soon cuddled up together.

Leonie took the joey to Jirrahlinga Koala and Wildlife Sanctuary, where he was looked after until he was old enough to live independently. Tehree Gordon, the owner of the sanctuary, was very impressed with Rex's efforts, noting that Rex was so gentle that the joey wasn't even distressed, which is pretty rare for such an interaction.

Rex's actions show that good training can help dogs to tolerate the native animals with which they share their environments.

CRABBY CROWDS

Christmas Island isn't quite what you might expect – you won't find many presents or formal lunches there. Two-thirds of the island is a national park, home to many unique animals and plants. Admittedly, there are no reindeer, but you may see an interesting red creature or two ... *million.*

One of the most incredible things about Christmas Island is the forest-to-coast migration of the tens of millions of red crabs that live there. This is, obviously, a whole lot of crabs.

At the beginning of the wet season, they head to the water to spawn. Once they reach the shore, the males dig a cosy, romantic burrow before they're joined by their lady crab friends. After a nice evening together, the males go for a swim and then head back to the forest. The ladies produce eggs three days after the rendezvous, and then hang around the burrow for twelve or thirteen days while they get ready for the tide to rise. The seawater eventually reaches the burrows and hits the eggs. Then the baby crabs hatch and are washed out to sea. They cruise about in the water for a month or so, developing through various stages until they gradually make it back to shore. The tiny crustaceans then scuttle into the forest until it's their turn to return to the beach.

These crabs are well looked after. Parks Australia employees on the island have amazing strategies in place to protect the crabs from cars and humans during their migration. But the crabs do have one enemy that Parks Australia can't help them with: the yellow crazy ant. (That's not a lie, it's what they're called.) These ants shoot acid into the crabs' eyes (still true), which can be fatal. It's like a comic book: the tiny, acid-shooting demon ant is the arch-nemesis of the smiley Christmassy crab. We know who we're barracking for. 🦀

SIRI the CHEETAH CUB & IRIS the PUPPY

Siri isn't just adorable – she's also an important addition to the vulnerable coalition of cheetahs living at Taronga Zoo in Sydney. (There are some pretty odd collective nouns out there, but 'coalition' is up there with the weirdest.)

Cheetahs are incredible animals: they are the fastest land animal, capable of reaching speeds of up to 120 kilometres per hour, which is faster than you're allowed to drive in most Australian states. They're good at hunting, but they're not so good at defending themselves against predators. They're also not doing so great on the survival front at the moment: deadly threats to their habitat, competition for food and the illegal pet trade are having a significant impact on the wild population. Plus, while cheetah mums can have up to nine cubs at once, most of those in the wild don't survive until adulthood, and cheetahs don't breed well in captivity.

With so much at stake, the keepers at Taronga Zoo faced a tough problem when they realised that Siri's mum was showing signs of rejecting her cub. Usually, cheetah litters contain three to five cubs, but Siri was born without a single sibling. In the wild, solo cubs are often abandoned because they have less chance of survival, but luckily Siri had the keepers on her side. They decided to do everything they could to make sure Siri survived and that she'd grow up to be healthy and well socialised. So they got her a puppy! Iris was a big, strong retriever–mastiff cross who could hold her own against the young cat. Siri was initially cautious around Iris, and was bestowed the title of 'drama queen' by the zookeepers for squealing at the sight of the puppy. However, their relationship steadily developed to the point where keepers spotted the two snuggling on cooler days.

While it would have been better if Siri could have been raised by her mum, having a companion like Iris aided Siri's development by ensuring that she learnt the natural social skills she needed to thrive. Plus, she got to be one half of an adorable pair.

As for Iris, she enjoyed her time socialising with the young cheetah and then happily retired.

BUM-BREATHING TURTLE

The Fitzroy River turtle is known for its streamlined approach to life: by combining various bodily functions into one opening, it can breathe through its bum.

The opening, called the cloaca, is located below the turtle's tail and has specialised gills that allow the turtle to stay underwater for up to twenty-one days at a time.

These cute and quirky reptiles are only found in the Fitzroy River Basin. Sadly, because newborns have a low survival rate, due to predation by feral foxes, cats and pigs, the Fitzroy River turtle population is at risk. Conservation efforts in recent years have been made to protect their nests from grubby predator paws. Hopefully, this will boost the turtle population and they can, uh, breathe a little easier.

PEBBLE the JOEY

Pebble the kangaroo was rescued by Ballarat Wildlife Park after she became an orphan at seven months old.

Because she was too young to join the mob of kangaroos without her mum to help her out, she was adopted by Luke, one of the keepers at the wildlife park. The two became inseparable. She followed him around during the day and slept inside his house at night, even curling up in her makeshift pouch to watch *Animal Kingdom* in the evenings.

Sometimes it's not in a kangaroo's best interests to be released back into the wild after the animal has developed a close relationship with a human. At a lot of rescue parks, there's a mob of similarly raised roos that have a semi-wild, semi-tame lifestyle.

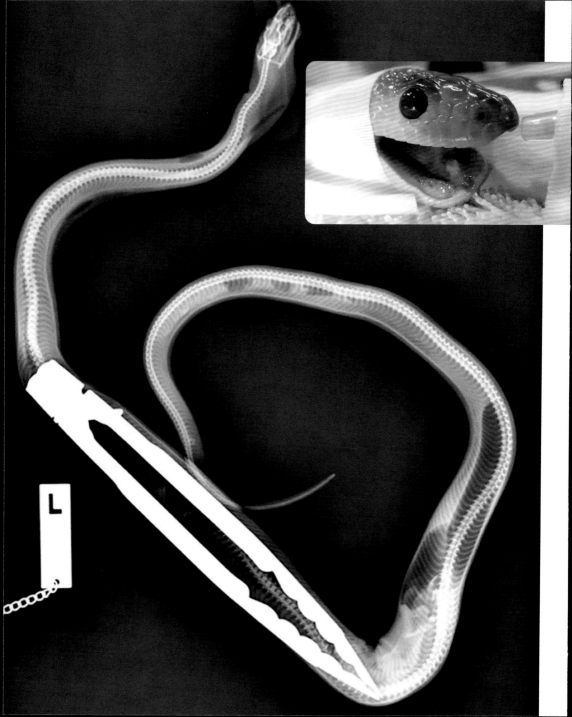

the TERRIBLE BBQ GUEST

Snakes are one of those dangerous animals that are used to prove that Australia is trying to kill its inhabitants. And yeah, there are a lot of snakes and many are venomous, but more Australians die each year being stung by bees than bitten by snakes.

So while it makes sense to be wary of things that can hurt you (like snakes, but also, you know, cars and bees), snakes aren't necessarily out to attack you – and sometimes, they're adorable and silly, like Winston the python.

Winston really should be more careful about what he eats. His owner was feeding him his usual meal of rats (yum) with a pair of barbecue tongs when the python gulped down the metal tongs instead.

Even though snakes can usually regurgitate their food whole, the tongs were just too big – they were about one-third the length of Winston's body and were pretty seriously stuck in his stomach. Dr Oliver Funnell, a vet at the University of Adelaide, had to perform surgery on the python to remove the implement. Happily, Winston the silly snake recovered, and hopefully he's learnt a lesson about biting off more than he can chew.

CHIP the EMU HERDER

Chip was a smart kelpie with a rather unusual job. He lived on a farm in Kerang, Victoria – an emu farm, in fact – and his work involved rounding up a flock of 2500 emus every day. He was such a natural with these intimidating birds that he could gather the huge flock much more quickly than his fellow farm workers, Jeff and Bev, ever could.

As well as being an Australian icon, emus are bred for their meat and fat, which gets turned into an oil that's said to have therapeutic properties.

Emu farms aren't very common in Australia, partly because they're quite expensive to establish, so Chip's job of protecting the emus and making sure they didn't escape was a rare and important one.

Chip was very gentle with the emu chicks because he knew they were only babies. When the birds got bigger, though – much bigger than Chip himself – he wasn't afraid to boss them around. Sometimes, the emus gave him a painful peck, but, ever the professional, Chip never responded with anger. He knew that patience and the ability to withstand such rude behaviour were the key selection criteria for the role of emu-herder.

Chip also played games with his flock of emus. He would poke his feet underneath the fence of the paddock for the big birds to try to peck. (Gee, fun game, Chip.)

Jeff says he was very grateful for Chip's help, and reckons he really was a top dog. 🐕🦤

CUTEST COUPLE AWARD

Anzac the kangaroo and Peggy the wombat are adoptive siblings with a difference – and it's about as heart-melting as it gets. Both Anzac's and Peggy's mums were killed after being hit by cars, but these little orphans were lucky enough to be saved by people who were careful to check the pouches for joeys.

Anzac was a few months old when he was rescued and brought to the Wild About Wildlife Rescue Centre in Victoria. Peggy had already been living at the shelter for a while, and because the young marsupials shared similar body movements and heartbeats, the staff thought it would be a good idea to pair them up. The adorable duo got along swimmingly, and they even shared a pouch at bedtime.

While their different body shapes and sizes meant they couldn't share the pouch for long – Anzac grew bigger faster and kangaroos are pretty big animals – having that closeness and comfort as young joeys helped them grow healthy, strong and confident.

About a year later, Peggy was ready to be released back into her natural habitat (with the workers at Wild About Wildlife keeping an eye on her from a distance).

Kangaroos mature a little slower than wombats, so Anzac needed more time before he could be released. But his early friendship with Peggy gave the cheeky, happy roo the best possible chance to grow and survive in the wild.

It's pretty hard for kangaroos to move backwards. Their big feet and heavy tail make them great at leaping forward, but totally unable to reverse. Apparently, the idea that they can only move forward is the reason that the kangaroo (and the emu, who suffers from a similar affliction) was chosen for the Australian coat of arms, which is accompanied by the motto 'Advance Australia'. Get it?

On average, male eastern grey kangaroos weigh in at around 50 to 65 kilograms and stand up to 2 metres tall. They live for six to twelve years in the wild. Wombats can grow to about a metre in length and weigh around 20 to 35 kilograms, and they usually live for about fifteen years. Even more interesting, wombats have cube-shaped poo and no one really knows why. It's a question we keep asking ourselves.

QUOKKAS
your new favourite animal

The quokka could well be the cutest animal on the entire planet. These cat-sized marsupials are friendly and pretty laid-back, and they look like they have a permanent smile on their chubby little faces.

Quokkas live in Western Australia, mostly on Rottnest Island and Bald Island, where they have become a serious tourist drawcard. As they have no natural predators on these islands, they've managed to build up relatively healthy populations – ones with an amazing lack of fear when it comes to the humans that visit them. Lately, they've been finding international fame by getting in on the selfie craze, sticking their grinning faces into other people's photos. These animals were born to rule the internet.

But before you start googling 'buy a quokka', keep in mind that they're not really pet material – on the rare occasions when these independent fellas get freaked out, they've been known to do some serious scratching with their long, clawed feet. Journalist Kenneth Cook learnt this the hard way when he tried to befriend a quokka by offering it a taste of his lunch, to which the quokka responded by falling into a dead faint. Mortified, and afraid that he'd poisoned the animal, Kenneth put the quokka into his backpack, hopped on his bike and peddled off in search of help. Unfortunately, the quokka started to revive and was not impressed by the undignified position it had been put into. It leapt out of the bag, scratching and screaming at Kenneth before latching onto his ear, until Kenneth peddled straight off a cliff and into the ocean. Luckily, neither of them suffered any long-term harm. So, no, quokkas aren't all sweetness and fun, but they're not going to gore you if you don't give them a biscuit. (Note: don't give them biscuits – it's bad for their digestion.)

Despite their happy life on the islands, on the mainland quokkas are threatened by introduced species such as foxes and cats. Land clearing has also limited their habitat, and it's all come together to mean that quokkas are now considered a vulnerable species. So, if we want to keep these cute little firecrackers around, it's important that we protect them – and remember to keep our lunches to ourselves.

did you know?

Quokkas open their mouths to pant when they're hot, which is part of the reason why they look so smiley.

LULU the SUPER-ROO

Lulu the hand-reared kangaroo clearly learnt a thing or two from watching re-runs of *Skippy*. In 2003, Lulu's carer Len was hit by a falling branch and knocked unconscious.

Things could have been pretty dire for Len if it wasn't for his trusty sidekick, a ten-year-old western grey who'd been rescued by the family as a joey. Lulu knew something was wrong, so she began 'barking' to draw attention to the situation. ('Barking' is a nice way to describe the noise kangaroos make when they sense danger – a sound not unlike someone snorting. Charming, eh?) After about fifteen minutes of Lulu's strange behaviour, the rest of the family went to see why she was so upset. After they found Lulu guarding an injured Len, he was rushed to hospital where he was treated and made a full recovery. Lulu was awarded the RSPCA National Animal Valour Award in 2004, which we think is well deserved. Her bond with Len indicates a very special, trusting relationship and shows that family is what you make it!

LONE GOAT on the LAM

Wategoat the one-horned goat belonged to a herd that once roamed free across the cliffs at Cape Byron. She was the only one left standing after rangers captured and relocated the rest.

In 2013, Wategoat was spotted stuck on a rocky outcrop at the base of the cape. Locals reported that she seemed to be injured and had not moved from her position for about two weeks.

The RSPCA planned a rescue mission. But Wategoat was understandably wary of the people who had whisked away the rest of her kin. Upon spotting the RSCPA team abseiling down the cliff, she displayed a burst of strength, jumping off the ledge and fleeing from her would-be saviours.

A lone horn was found a year after she was last seen. The horn is now displayed at the Cape Byron Lighthouse Museum, immortalising Wategoat's story.

the GREAT EMU WAR

Emus are terrifying creatures. When it comes to Australian animals, most people are scared of snakes, spiders, sharks, dingoes and crocodiles – and that's all well and good, but surely we should be more concerned by the fact that one of the animals on our coat of arms is basically a feathered dinosaur?

Emus are the second-largest bird in the world (after the ostrich), reaching heights of nearly two metres. Their legs are among the strongest of any animal, and while they can't fly, they can run incredibly fast (around fifty kilometres per hour). They'll attack you if you get too close to their chicks, they make really scary noises, their eyes will haunt your dreams and they can even swim – so there are few methods of escape if one's after you. They're also virtually bulletproof, as the Australian Army discovered in the 1930s after declaring war on a rogue emu population.

Back in 1932, some rowdy emus – and by some, we mean around twenty thousand – made the people in the central districts of Western Australia mighty uneasy. Taking over the town, wrecking fences, eating crops, picking fights at the pub: these emus needed to be shown who's boss. The population of Campion, Western Australia, included a large number of recently returned soldiers from World War I, and they knew just what would sort those pesky emus out: machine guns. The veterans had a chat to the Minister of Defence about their idea to combat the emus, and the minister eventually agreed to let the humans take them on. This decision to kill a big flock of birds became an actual official military operation, and the soldiers headed into the affray happy in the thought that the emus' feathers would make a rather dashing addition to their dress hats.

The humans gave it a red-hot go. They smashed out around ten thousand rounds of ammo, but reports indicated that they only managed to kill about one thousand birds. Apparently, the birds were smarter, faster and trickier to shoot than anticipated. They would move out of range and hide among trees before the soldiers could aim, but, more worryingly, even when they had clearly been hit by bullets they didn't seem to notice.

After several attempts to eradicate the birds, the army gave up. Yep, the emus had won. The leader of the mission, Major Meredith, said, 'If we had a military division with the bullet-carrying capacity of these birds, it would face any army in the world. They could face machine guns with the invulnerability of tanks.'

Emus: 1

Humans: 0

AN ODD
LITTLE COMBO

Oddball the maremma was one special canine; in 2005, she was given the important task of protecting a whole island's worth of tiny penguins.

It all started because the little penguins on Middle Island, south of Warrnambool in Victoria, were under threat. Foxes were sneaking across to the island during low tide to feast on innocent penguins, and humans were visiting in increasing numbers and crushing the penguins' sandy burrows. In five years, the number of penguins on Middle Island had dropped from two hundred to around ten. A number of interventions were introduced to protect the penguin population, and while closing the island to the public solved the human problem, foxes don't tend to be quite so respectful of 'Do not enter' signs.

Maremmas are originally from Italy, where they were bred to protect flocks of sheep from sneak wolf attacks. They're such skilled and disciplined protectors that they've also been trained to protect birds – though by birds we're generally talking about nothing more exotic than chickens.

However, local organic egg farmer Allan Marsh, known as 'Swampy', realised that these dogs – particularly Oddball, his fox-deterring pooch – might be the solution to the Middle Island penguins' problem. Because Oddball had been so well trained, she was able to take her chook knowledge and, with a bit of imagination, apply it to the strange, formally dressed little birds that needed her help.

Oddball's new position worked a treat, and her success was enough to encourage the council to train two more dogs, Eudy and Tula, to work on the island for the six months of the year that the penguins live there. Happily, since the maremmas began guarding the penguins, not a single fox kill has been recorded, and the penguin population is back up to around 180.

Though Oddball has since moved on to the big chook run in the sky, you can learn more about her through the 2015 family film she inspired, titled *Oddball* in her honour.

COCKATOOS PREFER BLONDES

A cockatoo in Queensland only likes people with long blonde hair (which is pretty judgemental for a bird with a pink Mohawk). Poya, the Major Mitchell's cockatoo, was not at all keen on Tom Patterson, the new zookeeper who was dropping by to feed her every day, and he started copping a bit of attitude from her – something that had never happened to any of Poya's previous (blonde, female) keepers.

Clearly something about the change of zookeepers was so upsetting to Poya that there was just no getting around it. After eight months of struggling with the temperamental bird, Tom began to wonder if his hairdo might be the problem. He jokingly tried on a blonde wig in an attempt to soothe the bird, and it seemed to do the trick – Poya found him much more to her taste. The other birds have also warmed more to Tom now that he's rocking his Gwyneth Paltrow do, so he's been donning the new look for every visit to the feathered fashion police.

SUDO & SIESTA

Siesta the donkey foal was only a little tacker when she was born two weeks early. But she was still one of the cutest baby animals around. And made even cuter by the fact that her best friend was Sudo the dog.

Sudo treated Siesta like her own baby, despite the donkey being quite a bit larger than the average puppy. Sudo and Siesta's owner, donkey breeder Linda Jay, said that the two were as close as can be, and they even snuggled down and slept together. Luckily, Siesta's biological mum was an open-minded donkey and didn't get jealous or overly protective of her foal. As Sudo has never been anything but gentle and affectionate with her young friend, it's clear Siesta's mum has nothing to worry about.

Donkeys and dogs both like living in packs and neither are particularly fussy about the species of that pack, so these two were more than happy to find that special friendship with each other.

KOALAS in MITTENS

While koalas are always cute – as is anything wearing mittens – the story behind these photos isn't all happy. Environments full of gum trees (the usual home for eucalyptus-loving koalas) are prone to bushfires, and the chilled-out marsupials regularly fall victim to these devastating natural disasters.

During bushfires, koalas often sustain burns to their paws, making it painful or even impossible for them to climb trees in order to feed, rest and sleep. Sore paws also make it painful for them to get away from predators.

After one such devastating bushfire, the International Fund for Animal Welfare (IFAW) put a call out for members of the public to sew and donate koala mittens made of soft cotton. These would help to protect the animals' paws while they healed. It's a gorgeous solution to a devastating issue, and has allowed the koalas to be returned safely and healthily to their native habitats.

Because this method of helping was so appealing, IFAW were quickly inundated with a substantial number of koala mittens, and at the time of writing the organisation is not in need of any more. You can check the IFAW website for specific methods of helping out animals in times of emergency, and donations are always helpful and welcome.

did you know?

Koalas have fingerprints that look suspiciously similar to human fingerprints. They're so similar that it's practically impossible to tell the difference between a koala's prints and a person's. Weird, right? And kind of scary – just think how many unsolved burglaries could actually have been committed by koalas ...

LURCHING
LORIKEETS

Since 2010, a weird illness has been hitting the lorikeet population of Darwin. A huge number of the parrots are stumbling around and crashing into things, or falling out of trees before passing out – basically being obnoxious drunks.

The sloshed birds were picked up off the side of the road and taken to wildlife centres and animal hospitals to recover from their hangovers. While this looks kind of funny, it's a bit of a worry for the veterinary community as no one knows what's making the lorikeets act so toasted. For a while it was assumed to be fermented fruit, but then it was thought to be a nasty seasonal virus. (A good excuse to keep in mind.) While no one enjoys a hangover, these birds can die from their benders because the illness affects their respiratory tracts. They are also much more likely to make poor decisions that leave them more vulnerable to predators (and more likely to pick fights with their mates and sing 'Khe Sanh' at karaoke).

SEALPRANO

Benny the long-nosed fur seal, named after Bennelong Point, decided in 2014 that he preferred a cultured lifestyle and settled in on some steps at the Sydney Opera House. Despite all the action in da house, Benny is a regular visitor and there are more than enough fish in the harbour to keep him well fed. It's also the perfect spot to sunbake and belt out some arpeggios while digesting lunch.

It's not very common for seals to live so close to humans, but Benny's comfort in the environment is thought to be a positive sign and might even encourage other seals to move to the area. Their movement to the mainland is also a good indication that the fur seal population is slowly but steadily recovering from its near-extinction in the 17th century.

Everyone's on board with welcoming the new resident, and the steps have been blocked off to give the seal a little bit of privacy as he listens to the music coming from the Opera House. He's generally a fan of classical music, but also enjoys the occasional stand-up comedy gig. You can also 'talk' to a Benny chatbot on the Sydney Opera House Facebook page!

a WOMBAT in my DRAWER

Kenny the wombat was rescued as a joey after his mum was killed by a car. He was bruised, and his nose and paws were damaged, but otherwise he was very lucky to have been protected in his mum's pouch.

The little joey was taken to the Australian Reptile Park in Somersby, New South Wales, and was bottle-fed by Tim Faulkner, the park's manager. As Kenny grew into a plump young wombat, he became more and more mischievous. While he still slept in a makeshift pouch indoors to keep warm and safe at night, like all teenagers he enjoyed pushing the boundaries, so he started exploring different areas of the house in search of good spots to take a nap. He found somewhere especially warm and comfortable in his caretaker's bedroom: the clever joey learnt how to nudge open the sock drawer to get to its soft and snuggly insides. He'd climb in (eventually – it'd take him a while because he was only little and not terribly coordinated) before making himself a hollow and falling fast asleep.

With all the rest he was getting, his caretakers hoped Kenny would be strong enough to return to the wild and live with other wombats, although it's unlikely he would find such a comfortable bed ever again. After all, burrows have got nothin' on socks. But then a startling discovery was made: Kenny was allergic to grass, which is only what wombats eat! Thankfully, Kenny received great treatment at the park. His life has been drama-free ever since, and has involved a lot of naps.

The wildlife park workers actively encourage people to stop and check the pouches of injured wildlife and make sure that little ones like Kenny have the best chance at survival. They also ask people to take note of the local injured wildlife hotline numbers in the areas that they're driving through. 🐗

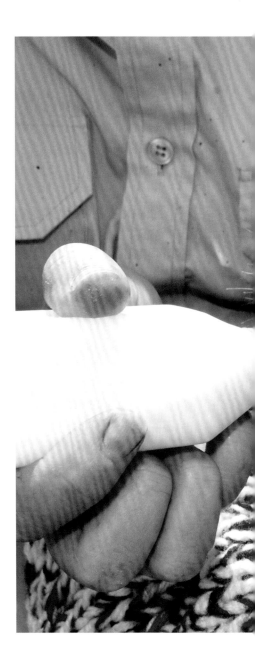

DONKEY GUARD

Dingoes and feral dogs had repeatedly attacked and killed Majella Rayment's young calves, and she was becoming increasingly frustrated. So she decided to hire the ultimate security guard: a baby donkey.

Donkeys are great guardian animals that keep predators, such as dingoes, away. They really don't like dogs and are happy to take them on in a fight. Little Dora has been entrusted with taking care of her new friend, Diego. Majella bottle-reared the donkey, who now seems like quite a mature young jenny. She's very protective of Diego and gets worried when he's out of her sight, which is a good sign for Diego's survival. Majella can rest easy knowing her calf is in good hands (or, you know, hooves).

Even though Dora is only close friends with Diego, her presence in the paddock is enough to protect the rest of the herd from dingo attacks. She is by far one of the best security guards around.

EMBARRASSING DADS

Samson the poodle may look like the ultimate daggy dad, but his surrogate kids don't seem to mind. He's an incredibly kind and lovely carer who's willing to foster any orphaned animal that comes his way.

He lives at the Jirrahlinga Sanctuary in Geelong, and he has helped to raise kangaroo and wombat joeys, as well as a litter of eleven dingo puppies. The curly-haired poodle takes it all in his stride.

Despite appearing interminably silly, poodles are actually pretty awesome dogs. They're very intelligent but also eager to please, they're capable of independent thought and love to help out their owners. Their unique coats have only one layer of fur, which means they're hypo-allergenic. Plus, they have webbed feet, so they're awesome at swimming: all things that add up to make Samson a wonderful dad.

The healthy, happy dingo puppies came from a conservation rescue facility in Victoria. Their time with Samson at Jirrahlinga is intended to help them to become socialised with humans and other animals, but while Samson is extremely well mannered, he probably won't be able to pass all of his good training on to his adopted kids. Dingoes may be able to interbreed with our pet pups, but they are a separate species to both wolves and domestic dogs. They've got some pretty wild and aggressive instincts that are impossible to train out. Still, it is possible to influence their behaviour to a point, and the hope is that Samson will help to bridge the gap between these cute young pups and their human keepers.

did you know?

Dingoes are considered a pest in some parts of Australia, but in other parts they are a protected species. Their continuation as a species is threatened because of their ability to breed with other dogs, which dilutes their unique characteristics. This reinforces the need for feral dog populations to be contained. (So here's a friendly reminder to desex your dogs to avoid contributing to this issue.)

MANDY & MANDY to the RESCUE

Mandy the goat and Mandy the border collie might be an unlikely rescue team, but they worked together to save the life of their owner, a farmer called Noel Osborne. 78-year-old Noel was working on his farm when a cow knocked him into a cow pat – which isn't even the worst part of the story, because he also broke his hip. He couldn't move and there was no one around to hear him calling for help.

Noel may have been unoriginal in his choice of pet names, but Mandy and Mandy still did all they could to help him through the ordeal: Mandy (the goat) let Noel drink her milk, which meant he stayed hydrated, and Mandy (the dog) stuck by Noel's side, keeping him warm overnight.

After five whole days, some of Noel's friends stopped by and found him. They called an ambulance – the only thing Mandy and Mandy couldn't do. He wasn't in good shape, but he was still alive, thanks to his two dedicated saviours. Mandy is a pretty handy animal to have around! And so is, uh, Mandy.

ESCAPEES

It seems that the orangutans in our zoos saw all the fun our native animals were having and wanted some too! In 2015, two orangutans managed to escape their enclosures within two weeks of each other.

Orangutans are extremely smart, inquisitive and very good at getting around obstacles. But they're also unpredictable animals with enough strength to cause serious damage. So when Malu the Sumatran orangutan got out of his enclosure at Melbourne Zoo, it sent the whole place into lockdown. It took an hour for the hairy escapee to be apprehended and returned to his enclosure. (*And* he tried it again in 2019!)

Two weeks after Malu's first escape and on the other side of the country, it was Teliti's turn to explore the world outside her Perth Zoo enclosure. The curious young ape managed to climb a shade cloth and jump out onto the boardwalk, mingling with her fans like a real celebrity. But it wasn't long before she decided that the human world wasn't all it was cracked up to be and returned, unharmed, to her safe space.

MOCHA & RUSTY

Mocha the Hungarian vizsla–labrador cross and Rusty the grey appaloosa from Pimpinio in western Victoria have an odd but lovely friendship. Ever since Mocha was a pup, the pair have been rather fond of each other. In their younger days, the two best mates would muck around together as if their size difference was nothing. Rusty the horse happily let Mocha lick his eyes and eyelashes, and Mocha didn't mind Rusty chewing on her ears and neck – which sounds like a pretty creepy relationship, but both of them were okay with it.

The pair played chasey for hours on end, throwing in the odd 'wizzy-dizzy' when Rusty would pick Mocha up by her collar to lift her a little way off the ground. Even though Mocha would sometimes cheekily try to lure Rusty towards the electric fence and give her companion a bit of a shock, Rusty was always careful not to hurt his buddy. 'Mocha would let Rusty know on the occasions he did get too rough – she'd yell, "Rough!"' says their owner, Helen Coutts.

In 2013, Mocha got quite sick with toxoplasmosis, a disease spread through cat faeces. (Mocha would like to warn other dogs that while eating poo may seem like a harmless jaunt, it can have disastrous consequences that take a while to recover from.) Her illness significantly affected her balance, movement and confidence, and she became slightly apprehensive about playing with Rusty. Horses are great at interpreting body language, and Rusty took Mocha's changed behaviour in his stride, adapting to the new rules of their relationship. Their interactions became a lot more chilled out, and the pair began to take leisurely walks around the paddock instead of their usual high-intensity activities.

Rusty's understanding helped Mocha get back to her old self, and that really is the kind of mate you want to be around when you're going through a tough time.

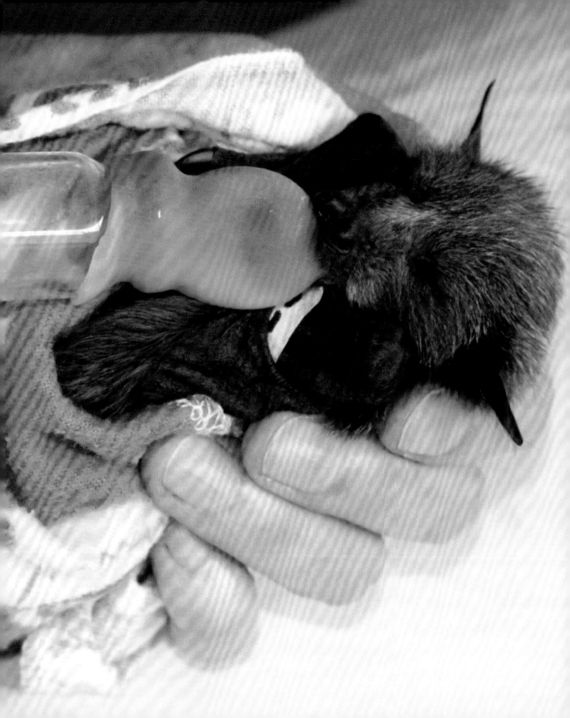

HEATWAVE

In November 2019, an extreme heatwave in Cairns, Queensland, tragically caused the deaths of over twenty-three thousand spectacled flying foxes despite volunteers' best efforts.

Because of the time of year, many of the bats were mothers with suckling pups, which made them particularly vulnerable to the severe heat. Incredibly, hundreds of the baby bats survived, and wildlife volunteers managed to rescue them.

The volunteers from WIRES gave the pups hydrating injections before transporting them to makeshift emergency hospitals. Because the little bats were so young, they needed to be bottle-fed around the clock to ensure their survival. Almost all of the pups lived, which shows the positive impact that dedicated rescue teams like WIRES can have on native species and the ongoing importance of keeping these organisations well resourced.

Tragically, the 2019 heatwave wiped out about one-third of the bat population. Another heatwave in 2020 also caused significant damage to bat colonies in other areas of Australia.

But there is hope to be had. An atmospheric cooling system made up of aerial sprinklers was tested in Bendigo's Rosalind Park, home to a breeding colony of grey-headed flying foxes. The sprinkler system had positive results: no flying fox deaths were recorded in the test zone. Plus, the bats seem to be total fans (pun intended) of their new cooling showers, and the droplets also help keep the ferns and other flora healthy and green.

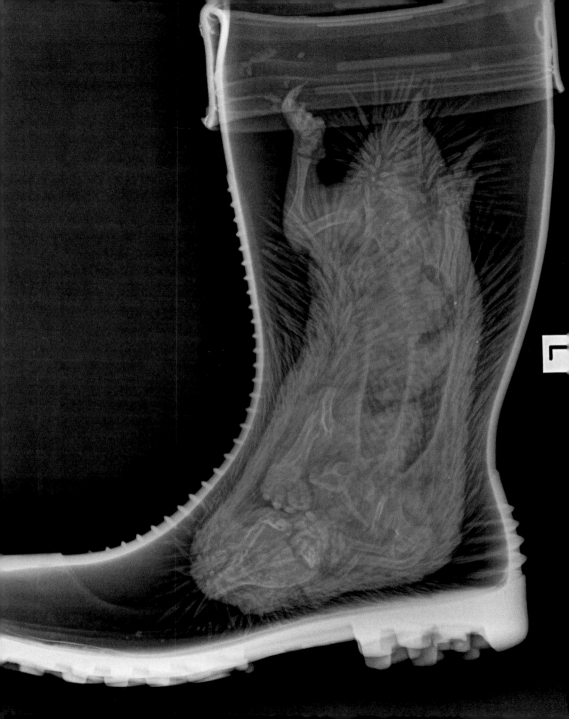

ECHIDNA vs GUMBOOT,
gumboot wins

Echidnas are one of the oldest surviving species of mammal on the planet, so you'd think that they'd have developed heaps of innate wisdom to aid their survival and stop them from making dumb mistakes. But apparently that's not the case, and sometimes their decision-making leaves a bit to be desired.

Take, for example, this echidna who thought it was a good idea to have a snooze in a gumboot. The silly little guy was feeling worn out, and like any echidna, all he wanted was a nice warm burrow to nap in. And what cosier burrow could you find than an item of farming footwear? Getting into the thick, rubbery boot was easy, but because of his spikes and the limited space to perform a U-turn, the echidna was soon trapped. An echidna's natural defence is to roll into a ball to protect itself from stressful situations, but this strategy worked against him and only served to wedge him in further. Whoops!

Luckily, the gumboot's owner noticed that there was something awry with his footwear, and he took his spiky boot to the Ark Animal Hospital in Darwin. The vet was able to do some cobbling and free the animal from its rubbery prison, and fortunately the echidna was completely healthy after his ordeal – if a tad embarrassed.

did you know?

While echidnas have a lot in common with other mammals, it's their reptilian characteristics that (along with their fellow monotreme, the platypus) makes them special in the animal world. Echidnas have the lowest body temperature of any mammal and, like reptiles, they have a cloaca – a single opening for reproduction, defecation and urination. Combine that with the fact that they lay eggs and their beaks have electroreceptors to detect their insect prey, and you've got one weird critter.

the EMU who thinks SHE'S a COW

Louie the emu was rescued in Aramac, Queensland, as a little chick, and she was raised alongside calves on grazier Margaret House's property.

Since then, Louie's lived a happy life, but has never really got her head around the fact that she's an emu; the confused bird has always identified far more strongly with the cows she hangs out with, and considers herself a key player in the herd.

Louie formed a somewhat romantic attachment to Margaret's Brahman bull, and the pair spend most of their time together. Louie even likes to take a nap in the sun with her beloved.

Unfortunately, she's quite possessive, and her bullfriend isn't allowed near any of the cows – which has caused a bit of a problem for Margaret's herd. Louie isn't worried about that, though, because she's too busy monopolising the bull's time. When you know, you know.

the EMU who thinks HE'S a HORSE

Emu the emu would much rather be a horse. About eight years ago, when he was a rather young bird, he packed up and moved in with the Alice Springs police horses, and he liked horsing around so much that he decided to stick with the band.

While Emu can come and go as he pleases, he's made his preferences very clear – mainly by strongly objecting to the many attempts that have been made to return him to a more typical environment. Senior Sergeant Edwards reckons that Emu has 'taken on the equine lifestyle', and he eats and gallops with the horses. He's helpful when it comes to desensitising the horses, but less helpful when it comes to legitimate police business, and he doesn't realise that he isn't as valuable to the force as he believes. Some of the horses accepted the new recruit, but others were, according to Melinda, 'not so keen'. None of them appreciate the casual rump-pecking that Emu enjoys. And under no circumstances will he be getting a badge.

the EMUS who think THEY'RE PEOPLE

Emus generally aren't too keen on living with a lot of humans – we're always showing them nice food and then shouting when they take it. But just like us, now and then they feel the need for a change of scene.

In late 2013, around fifty emus waltzed into Longreach, Queensland, like they owned the place. While most of the residents were happy to welcome the visitors, the birds could be annoying: they refused to follow road rules and had no regard for the aesthetics of people's gardens. But because they're huge and somewhat terrifying birds, they pretty much had free rein. The mayor, Joe Owens, acknowledged that they were causing 'a bit of a drama' but pragmatically realised there wasn't much to be done.

In 2019, the town once again witnessed mobs of emus coming into town in search of food and water due to the extended drought conditions. Locals were unfazed, peacefully coexisting with their fellow feathered citizens. Longreach even has an unofficial driving rule: give way to emus.

CASTAWAY

Sophie Tucker is a pretty incredible dog with a pretty incredible story. In 2008, Sophie the blue heeler went for a boat trip with her human family, Jan and Dave Griffith. During their cruise the day started to turn dark; the wind picked up, and the waves got bigger and choppier. When Dave had his back turned to check something on the boat, Sophie fell over the side. The waves were so rough that Jan and Dave couldn't see where their poor hound had fallen, and they had to turn back to shore without her, devastated at losing their much-loved pet.

But Sophie wasn't keen on calling it a day. Amazingly, she somehow swam five nautical miles in shark-infested waters and made it to St Bees Island, off the coast of Mackay. Even though dogs are good swimmers, it's pretty uncommon for one to last for more than half an hour in the water; they struggle to float and they have to move constantly to keep their heads above water. The weather, too, was less than ideal, so it's an incredible feat that Sophie made it to shore. Not only that, but the pooch also managed to find water and food and survived on the island for about five months. She certainly wasn't a favourite of the island's locals after she started honing her hunting skills on their baby goats.

Four months after their beloved pet's disappearance, Jan and Dave heard that a dog fitting Sophie's description had been found on the island, so the next time the ranger's boat came to the mainland, the Griffiths were waiting for it. Their hope was rewarded when they saw a worn-out but very excited Sophie on board.

Sophie returned to the comforts of domestic life quite happily, but her skills suggest that she'd be a real contender for a series of *Dog Survivor*. (Million-dollar idea, right?)

KANGAROO PAWS

In January 2016, bushfires razed parts of Western Australia. While you could replace '2016' with any year and 'Western Australia' with most Australian states and this statement would still stand, the frequency of fires in Australia doesn't make them any less devastating to the people or the wildlife that are mostly left to face the flames unprotected.

Around Yarloop, vets from Waroona Veterinary Clinic were overwhelmed by the number of animals injured by the fire, and they worked around the clock to try to save the local wildlife. Some creatures were luckier than others – like this little guy, whose special socks helped his burned paws to heal so that he was able to be returned to the remaining bushland. This photo of the poor joey was so sad and sweet that it went viral and brought some much-needed attention to the work that vets do in fire-damaged areas. Waroona's staff treated all sorts of wildlife, pets and livestock in order to help them recover from burns and smoke inhalation, and over several weeks the patients were able to get better as they rested in the clinic and even in the vets' backyards!

Despite the enormous damage to homes and property in the area, the local community still donated cash and food to help out the Waroona vets as they worked. It just goes to show that people can be incredibly generous when it comes to taking care of animals, even during the toughest times.

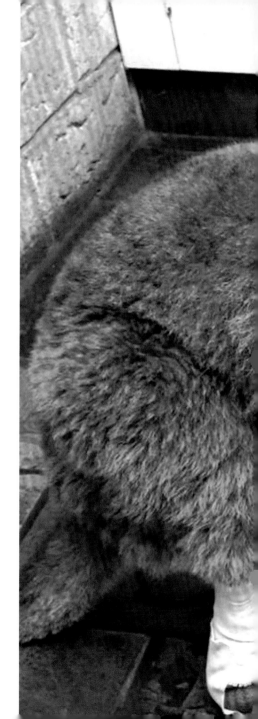

WOMBAT in a BEANIE

Plenty of kids (and adults for that matter) might dream of having a wombat for a pet, but Pinch the wombat proved that these stocky creatures can be as troublesome as they are lovable.

Pinch joined the Hume family after his mum was killed in a road accident. Alison and Eddy were going for a run at Dinner Plain in the Victorian high country when they came across a female wombat lying dead by the side of the Great Alpine Road, at a sharp corner known as Slippery Pinch. Alison checked the wombat's pouch and found a joey lying safe and warm, so she wrapped him up and took him home.

Pinch spent his early days with the Humes lying bundled in a beanie sitting on top of a warm stove. As he grew, the little wombat started exploring the farmland around the family home, wandering through the bush at the bottom of their property. The family decided to let him live outdoors so he could get a taste of wild wombat life, but he was still a part of the clan. (Though he was also rather camera shy, and would often give the kids a nip when they tried to make him pose for family photos.)

But as Pinch became more confident, he also got a lot cheekier: he liked to break into the house to steal dog food, leaving scratch marks all over the doors. One night, after yet another case of forced wombat entry, Eddy found himself chasing Pinch around the garden in the nude. The family decided it was finally time to help Pinch return to the wild for good, and the next morning they drove him up the road to set him free in the state forest.

Many years later, a senior wombat came to visit the Humes' back garden, but the old fella was unwell and died the next day. Ever since, the family has wondered whether it was Pinch coming home for one last visit.

the DOG DETECTIVE

Bear, the five-year-old Australian koolie dog, is part of a trained team that detects koalas by their scent and scat in bushfire-ravaged areas. Bear is sponsored by the International Fund of Animal Welfare (IFAW).

Bushfires are an ever-present threat to Australian wildlife. The country has striven to increase the efficiency of bushfire response, including search-and-rescue operations for injured and displaced animals. Enter the University of the Sunshine Coast Detection Dogs for Conservation – a team that uses detection dogs to help support animal welfare and protect Australia's unique habitat and species.

Bear and his fellow dog colleagues are all rescued animals and their team collaborates in many search-and-rescue operations, most significantly, the Black Summer fires. Between November 2019 and April 2020, Bear and his team were deployed to bushfire zones to search for koala survivors. They found more than one hundred injured, sick, dehydrated or starving koalas.

Bear is known for his obsessive-compulsive tendencies and boundless energy – ideal traits for an impeccable detection dog. Once the fire in an area subsides, it's time for action. Bear follows his nose and once he's caught a scent, he'll drop to the ground to signal 'follow me!' to his humans. Eventually, he will settle on a spot and refuse to move, indicating that it's time for the humans to scan the canopy for a koala.

The folks at IFAW believe his thought process is something like: 'Come on humans! Unbelievable. Can't you smell that? It's as obvious as a koala nose in the middle of a koala face!'

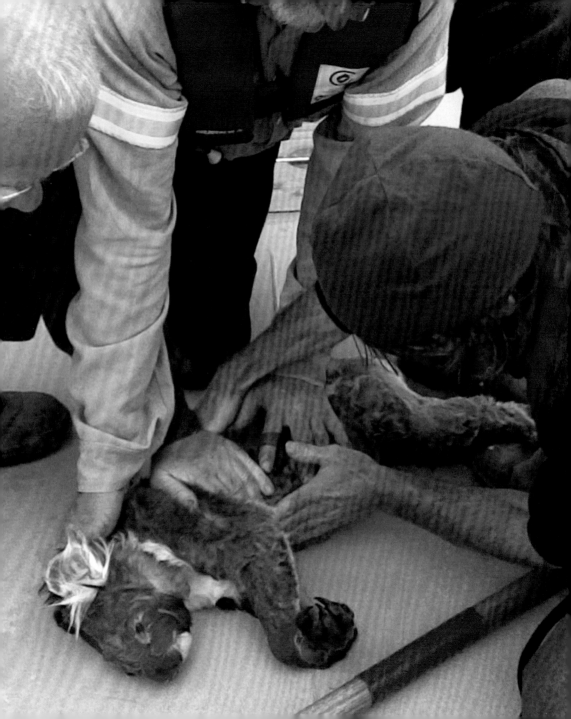

SOGGY BEAR

Even though the koalas in Portland, Victoria, seem to enjoy living near the coast – you can hear them shouting, 'How's the serenity?' to one another on a breezy afternoon – they're not real beach bums. Koalas aren't made to swim: their heavy coats quickly become waterlogged, so it can be difficult for them to get out of rivers and swimming pools. Or the sea.

The current of the ocean makes swimming a real challenge to poor, heavy koalas, and in 2008 the coast guards in Portland saved one lucky koala from drowning. By the time the guards realised that the furry creature in the distance wasn't just a dog having a dip, the not-quite-hydrodynamic marsupial wasn't breathing. The coast guards grabbed the soggy animal out of the ocean, drained the water out of him and performed CPR. They managed to resuscitate him and took him to the vet to be checked over. Luckily, he was okay after his ordeal, but this very fortunate koala should probably stick to the boardwalk from now on.

DISCO SPIDER

Arachnophobic? The solution to overcoming your fear might just lie in making the acquaintance of two of the prettiest, silliest spiders around.

Scientists have discovered ninety-two species of peacock spider (*Malatus*) so far, almost all in Australia. They tend to live on the ground and in small bushes, and each has its own unique appearance. These recently discovered species of peacock spider, known as sparklemuffin and skeletorus (nope, we're not joking), live across various parts of eastern Australia.

They're very beautiful: sparklemuffins' male members have blue and red bodies that rival any outfit you might see at a festival, and skeletorus' black and white markings would help them fit right in at a hip inner-city coffee shop.

But something they have in common, besides their seriously funky look, is some next-level dance floor skills to match. These spiders are only around half a centimetre long, and they can bust a move like you wouldn't believe. When a male spider is looking to attract a mate, he raises his third set of legs and waves it in the air like he just don't care, then spreads out his abdomen, flapping and wiggling it about to impress his beloved.

These little multi-eyed, multi-legged creatures are excellent beyond description, so we urge you to put down this book right now and type 'peacock spider dance' into YouTube. Quick. Your day will immediately be better.

AN ECHIDNAPPING

While animals can be pretty weird sometimes, people can be even weirder. Especially when they do things like break into a wildlife sanctuary and kidnap a monotreme.

It was a real shock when Piggie the echidna was snatched from her home at the Currumbin Wildlife Sanctuary. When her keepers discovered her missing one morning, the search began. But a few days later it seemed that the thieves had thought better of their crime and Piggie was found safe in the sanctuary, having been slipped under the fence. The culprits were finally arrested and they admitted it was all just a drunken prank. They'd broken in hoping to find a crocodile (because, sure), but when their search failed they'd taken Piggie instead.

Piggie's keepers reported she'd been very stressed by the experience, and could have been in real danger if she'd been kept for much longer. Luckily, she recovered from her ordeal, and a few months later gave birth to a very photogenic little puggle of her own!

PHOTO CREDITS

PUGGLE POWER – Leo the Echidna at Healesville Sanctuary © Rob Leeson / Newspix

SUPERDOG AND THE ORPHANED JOEY – Rex and the Joey © Craig Borrow / Newspix

CRABBY CROWDS – **Page 34:** Christmas Island Red Crab © John Tann. Accessed via Flickr, https://flic.kr/p/9FALBV; **Pages 36–37:** All photographs © Director of National Parks/Parks Australia

SIRI THE CHEETAH CUB – Cheetah Cub 'Siri' at Taronga Western Plains Zoo © Toby Zerna / Newspix

BUM-BREATHING TURTLE – Fitzroy River turtle (Rheodytes leukops) © Stephen Zozaya

PEBBLE THE JOEY – 'Pebble' the Kangaroo Joey © David Caird / Newspix

THE TERRIBLE BBQ GUEST – All photographs © Companion Animal Health Centre, University of Adelaide

CHIP THE EMU HERDER – Chip the Emu Dog © Craig Borrow / Diimex

CUTEST COUPLE AWARD – Orphaned Marsupials Make Friends at Rescue Centre © Robert Leeson / Newspix

QUOKKAS, YOUR NEW FAVOURITE ANIMAL – **Page 54:** World's happiest animal, Quokka © Jin Xiang, accessed via Flickr, https://flic.kr/p/oQpZdm; **Page 57:** Photograph © Ros Almond

LULU THE SUPER-ROO – Lulu and Len © Trevor Pinder / Newspix

LONE GOAT ON THE LAM – Wategoat © Sean O'Shea

THE GREAT EMU WAR – **Page 62:** Photograph © Christian Jansky, https://commons.wikimedia.org/wiki/File:Dromaius_novaehollandiae_head_02.jpg; **Page 65:** Photograph © John Robert McPherson, https://commons.wikimedia.org/wiki/File:Emu_Burke_River_floodplain_Boulia_Shire_Queensland_P1060859.jpg

ECHIDNA VS GUMBOOT – **Page 104:** Echidna in gumboot x-ray © The Ark Animal Hospital NT; **Pages 106–107:** Echidna in Gumboot © Elise Derwin / Newspix

THE EMU WHO THINKS SHE'S A COW – Emu and Cow © Adam Head / Newspix

THE EMU WHO THINKS HE'S A HORSE – Emu and Horse in Conversation © Australian Broadcasting Corporation Library Sales

THE EMUS WHO THINK THEY'RE PEOPLE – Emus in Longreach © Outback Pics, www.outbackpics.com.au

CASTAWAY – Sophie the Dog © Daryl Wright / Newspix

KANGAROO PAWS – All photographs © Waroona Veterinary Clinic

WOMBAT IN A BEANIE – All photographs © Alison Lester and Eddy Hume

THE DOG DETECTIVE – **Page 124:** Bear sits on the tailgate of his transport vehicle with his handler, USC Detection Dogs for Conservation researcher, Dr. Romane Cristescu. Photo © IFAW; **Page 125:** Bear at the scene after the catastrophic fires in Cooroibah. Photo © ficlarkphotography

SOGGY BEAR – Perform CPR © Portland Coast Guard. Thanks to Flotilla Commander Stephen Brown.

DISCO SPIDER – All photographs © Jürgen Otto

AN ECHIDNAPPING – Piggie and her Puggle © Tim Marsden / Newspix

ACKNOWLEDGEMENTS

Affirm Press wishes to thank everyone who willingly donated photographs to this collection of amazing animal stories.

Thanks to Australian Reptile Park and Aussie Ark; WIRES Northern Rivers; Wildlife Habitat, Port Douglas; IFAW; Parks Australia; Melbourne Museum; Phillip Island Nature Parks; Ballarat Wildlife Park; The Ark Animal Hospital, Northern Territory; Australian Volunteer Coast Guard Association, Portland; the University of Adelaide; Waroona Veterinary Clinic; and Debra Scott from Outback Pics for the generous donation of images. Special thanks to Dominca Mack, Mark Sawa, Max Orchard, Amanda Woodbine, Sue Ulyatt, Ashley Stewart, Helen Coutts, Clare Anderson, Narelle Spencer, Chelsea Pearson, Roland Pick, Diane Whatling, Mandy Hall, Stephen Brown and Vivienne Sykes for your time, patience and efforts locating the photographs for this book. We have also accessed images via Flickr and Wikimedia Commons, and we are extremely appreciative of photographers who release their images to the public domain.

Special thanks to Ros Almond for creating the majority of the stories, and Hannah White, Amelia Mouradian, Banpreet Shahi, Laura Franks and Vanessa Pellatt for their research and contributions.